www.ingramcontent.com/pod-product-compliance
Lightning Source LLC
Chambersburg PA
CBHW061942280526
45787CB00004B/1697
* 9 7 8 1 5 3 4 6 0 0 2 7 0 *